THE SCOTTISH OFFICE

SCOTLAND'S PARLIAMENT

Presented to Parliament by the Secretary of State for Scotland by
Command of Her Majesty
July 1997

Cm 3658

£6.50

More information on the Government's proposals is available on The Scottish Office devolution web site

http://www.scottish-devolution.org.uk

ISBN 0 10 136582 9

CONTENTS

The Government are pledged to clean up and modernise British politics. We are committed to a comprehensive programme of constitutional reform. We believe it is right to decentralise power, to open up government, to reform Parliament and to increase individual rights.

The elements are well known:

- a Scottish Parliament and a Welsh Assembly giving the people of Scotland and Wales more control over their own affairs within the United Kingdom;

- an elected Mayor and new strategic authority for London with more accountability in the regions of England;

- new rights for citizens with the incorporation into UK law of the European Convention on Human Rights;

- Freedom of Information;

- a referendum on the voting system for the House of Commons.

This White Paper marks a major step forward in the achievement of our proposals. It sets out our proposals for the Scottish Parliament, on which the people of Scotland will have the opportunity to vote in a referendum in the autumn. I will be campaigning strongly for a double "yes" vote in the forthcoming referendum.

Scotland is a proud historic nation in the United Kingdom and the plans we put forward in this White Paper will give it an exciting new role within the United Kingdom.

Tony Blair

TONY BLAIR

FOREWORD BY THE SECRETARY OF STATE FOR SCOTLAND

The Government's aim is a fair and just settlement for Scotland within the framework of the United Kingdom - a settlement which will be good both for Scotland and the United Kingdom. The Scottish Parliament will strengthen democratic control and make government more accountable to the people of Scotland.

Scotland will remain firmly part of the United Kingdom. Westminster will continue to be responsible for those areas of policy best run on a United Kingdom basis. These include foreign affairs, defence and national security and macro-economic and fiscal matters. It follows that the UK Government will continue to act in many areas of public life in Scotland but in future it will be the Scottish Parliament - working within the framework of the United Kingdom - which will be responsible for much of the business of government in Scotland.

The Scottish Parliament will reflect the needs and circumstances of all of the people of Scotland regardless of race, gender or disability. Scotland will no longer be the only democratic country with its own legal system but no legislature of its own.

With its new responsibilities, the Scottish Parliament will be in a position to encourage vigorous sustainable growth in the Scottish economy. Policies on health, housing and education will respond more directly to Scotland's needs. The Parliament will work to protect and develop our unique environment and natural and built heritage and to enrich our cultural inheritance.

Like many others, I have campaigned long and hard for a Scottish Parliament over the years. I have never doubted the importance of the issue or the difference that a Parliament will make.

This reform will not in itself solve the problem of resources or banish the dilemmas of government. What it can do is connect and involve people with the decisions that matter to them. It can bring a sense of ownership to political debate and a new confidence to our affairs.

The argument for change has been sustained through the difficult days. Now is the time for decision.

There should be no further delay. This White Paper sets out in practical detail the Government's plans to translate our manifesto commitments into a sound and durable constitutional settlement. It will be widely welcomed throughout Scotland. A referendum will be held on 11 September. The people of Scotland will make their choice. I am confident that there will be a resounding vote in favour of both propositions.

DONALD DEWAR

A SUMMARY OF THE PROPOSALS

What the
Scottish
Parliament can do

The Scottish Parliament will have law-making powers over a wide range of matters which affect Scotland. There will be a Scottish Executive headed by a First Minister which will operate in a way similar to the UK Government and will be held to account by the Scottish Parliament. The Scottish Parliament and Executive will be responsible for:

- **Health** including the National Health Service in Scotland and public and mental health;

- **Education and training** including pre-5, primary, secondary, further and higher education; and training policy and programmes;

- **Local government, social work and housing** including local government structure and finance; social work; the voluntary sector; housing policy; area regeneration; building control; and the statutory planning framework;

- **Economic development and transport** including responsibility for the economic development of Scotland; financial and other assistance and support for Scottish business and industry; promotion of trade and exports; inward investment; tourism; functions in relation to the energy sector; the administration of the European Structural Funds; and a range of road, rail, air, sea transport and inland waterways matters;

- **The law and home affairs** including most civil and criminal law and the criminal justice and prosecution system including police and prisons; fire services; legal aid; parole, the release of life-sentence prisoners and alleged miscarriages of justice; certain Crown, church, ceremonial and local government electoral matters; and civil defence and emergency planning;

- **The environment** including environmental protection policy and matters relating to air, land and water pollution; the natural and built heritage; and water supplies, sewerage, flood prevention and coastal protection;

- **Agriculture, fisheries and forestry** including The Scottish Office's existing responsibilities for promoting agriculture and fisheries in Scotland and those of the Forestry Commission in Scotland;

- **Sport and the arts** including the Scottish Sports Council, the Scottish Arts Council and the national institutions;

- **Research and statistics** in relation to devolved matters.

Scotland in the United Kingdom

The legislation setting up the Scottish Parliament will specify those powers which are reserved to the UK Parliament. These matters include the **constitution** of the United Kingdom; **UK foreign policy** including relations with Europe; **UK defence** and **national security**; the stability of the UK's **fiscal, economic and monetary system**; **common markets** for UK goods and services; **employment legislation**; **social security**; and most aspects of **transport safety and regulation.**

The new constitutional arrangements

Scotland will remain an integral part of the United Kingdom, and The Queen will continue to be Head of State of the United Kingdom. The UK Parliament is and will remain sovereign.

Scotland's MPs will continue to play a full and constructive part at Westminster. The number of Scottish seats will be reviewed.

The Secretary of State for Scotland will work with the new Scottish Parliament and represent Scottish interests within the UK Government.

The Scottish Executive and the UK Government will work closely together at both Ministerial and official level.

There will be arrangements for resolving disagreements about whether legislation is within the powers of the Scottish Parliament.

Relations with the European Union

Relations with the EU will remain the responsibility of the UK Government, but the Scottish Executive will be involved as closely as possible in UK decision-making on Europe.

Ministers of the Scottish Executive will participate in relevant meetings of the Council of Ministers and in appropriate cases could speak for the United Kingdom.

The Scottish Parliament will be able to scrutinise EU legislative proposals.

There will be a Scottish representative office in Brussels to further Scotland's interests and complement the role of UKREP.

The Scottish Executive will have an obligation to implement EU legislation on devolved matters. The UK Parliament will continue to have the ability to legislate to give effect to EU obligations in Scotland.

Relations with local government and other bodies

The Scottish Parliament will set the framework within which other Scottish public bodies - local government, non-departmental public bodies and health bodies - operate. The detailed arrangements will be for the Scottish Parliament and Scottish Executive to develop.

Financial arrangements

The financial framework for the Scottish Parliament will be closely based on existing arrangements for financing The Scottish Office, and will allow the Scottish Parliament to approve spending decisions in accordance with Scottish needs and priorities.

The control of local authority expenditure, non-domestic rates and other local taxation will be devolved to the Scottish Parliament.

Subject to the outcome of the referendum, the Scottish Parliament will be given power to increase or decrease the basic rate of income tax set by the UK Parliament by up to 3p. Liability will be determined by residence in Scotland. Income from savings and dividends will not be affected.

The Inland Revenue will administer any tax variation, with the Scottish Parliament meeting the administrative costs.

Electoral arrangements

The Scottish Parliament will consist of 129 members, 73 directly elected on a constituency basis, plus 56 additional members (7 from each of the 8 current European Parliament constituencies) allocated to ensure the overall result more directly reflects the share of votes cast for each party.

Eligibility to vote will be based on residency.

Parliamentary arrangements

Each Scottish Parliament will have a 4-year fixed term.

The Scottish Parliament is expected to adopt modern methods of working; and to be accessible and responsive to the needs of the public. Detailed arrangements will be left to the Scottish Parliament itself.

Making it happen

The Government are looking at options available in Edinburgh for the Scottish Parliament building.

The staff of the Scottish Executive will continue to be part of a unified Home Civil Service.

The annual running costs are estimated to be between £20 and £30 million a year i.e. about £5 per year per head of Scottish population.

Next steps

Scotland will be asked to vote on 11 September in a referendum on the proposals set out in this White Paper.

Following a positive referendum result, legislation to establish a Scottish Parliament will be brought forward as soon as possible.

Once the legislation has been enacted, elections to the Scottish Parliament will be held in the first half of 1999, and the Parliament will become fully operational in the year 2000.

CHAPTER 1

INTRODUCTION AND BACKGROUND

1.1   The Government are determined that the people of Scotland should have a greater say over their own affairs. With their agreement we will change the way Scotland is governed by legislating to create a Scottish Parliament with devolved powers within the United Kingdom. This Chapter sets out the historical background and developments since the 1970s.

Historical background

1.2   Following the Union of Crowns of Scotland and England in 1603, the Union of the Scottish and English Parliaments in 1707 created a Parliament of Great Britain meeting in London.

1.3   A Secretary of State for Scotland was appointed in the first post-union Government. After 1745 however no such appointment was made; and while responsibility for Scotland during the majority of the ensuing period lay with the Home Secretary, most of the effective political power was exercised by the Lord Advocate. This system lasted until 1885 when the office of Secretary for Scotland was created. The status of the office of Secretary for Scotland was enhanced in 1926 to that of Secretary of State. As the Secretary of State's responsibilities gradually increased, St Andrew's House in Edinburgh became the headquarters of The Scottish Office in 1939 and the functions of The Scottish Office in London were transferred to Edinburgh. In recent years, further administrative devolution to The Scottish Office has taken place, resulting in the addition of major functions such as industrial support, training, higher education and the arts.

Scotland Act 1978

1.4   During the 1970s, in the light of the deliberations of the Royal Commission on the Constitution (the Kilbrandon Commission), the then Labour Government brought forward proposals to establish a Scottish Assembly. In November 1977 a Scotland Bill providing for the establishment of a Scottish Assembly was introduced; it received its Royal Assent on 31 July 1978. The Act required that a referendum be held; and an amendment carried during its Parliamentary passage required that, if less than 40% of the electorate voted in favour of its provisions, an Order repealing the Act should be laid. The referendum was held on 1 March 1979. 1,230,937 voted in favour of an Assembly – a majority in excess of 77,000 – but this represented only 32.9% of the electorate; the Act was repealed by Order on 26 July 1979.

Recent developments

1.5 Since 1988, the cross-party campaign for change has been led by the Scottish Constitutional Convention, comprising Members of Parliament of the Labour and Liberal Democrat parties, Labour members of the European Parliament, local authorities, the STUC, business, church and civic groups and other political parties. The Convention's final report *Scotland's Parliament. Scotland's Right* which was published on St Andrew's Day, 1995 set out their proposals for a Scottish Parliament.

1.6 The Government have a manifesto commitment to a comprehensive programme of constitutional reform. In its scope, scale and significance this programme will bring about the most ambitious and far reaching changes in the British constitution undertaken by any Government this century. The aim is to make government more accessible, open and accountable. It includes devolution to Scotland and Wales; greater regional government for England and a strategic authority and elected mayor for London (subject to referendums); reforms to both Houses of Parliament; the incorporation of the European Convention of Human Rights into UK law; and a Freedom of Information Act. This comprehensive programme will give the United Kingdom a modern constitution fit for the 21st Century.

1.7 The manifesto promised legislation to allow the people of Scotland and Wales to vote in referendums to be held by the autumn of 1997 on proposals to be set out in White Papers. That legislation will shortly complete its passage through Parliament and this document is the White Paper on the basis of which the people of Scotland will be invited to make their historic choice.

CHAPTER 2

WHAT THE SCOTTISH PARLIAMENT CAN DO

2.1   The Government are committed to creating a Scottish Parliament which will extend democratic control over the widespread responsibilities currently exercised by The Scottish Office and other Scottish Departments. These have nearly 12,000 civil servants serving Scotland's needs. What is required is a more effective democratic framework. This Chapter sets out what will be devolved, and the roles of the Scottish Parliament and the new Scottish Executive.

2.2   The proposed settlement reflects the changes in The Scottish Office's responsibilities over the past 20 years and the Government's commitment to establish a Scottish Parliament with wide-ranging powers including some matters not currently discharged by The Scottish Office. Among the areas to be devolved, not included in the devolution proposals of the Scotland Act 1978, are economic development, financial and other assistance to industry, universities, training, forestry, certain transport matters, the police and the prosecution system.

The Scottish Parliament

2.3   The role of the Scottish Parliament will be to make laws in relation to devolved matters in Scotland. In these devolved areas, it will be able, by virtue of the devolution legislation, to amend or repeal existing Acts of the UK Parliament and to pass new legislation of its own in relation to devolved matters. It will also be able to consider and pass private legislation, promoted by individuals or bodies (for example local authorities) in relation to devolved matters.

2.4   All matters that are not specifically reserved - see Chapter 3 - will be devolved. Devolved matters over which the Scottish Parliament will have legislative power include:

Health

- **health** generally including overall responsibility for the National Health Service in Scotland and public and mental health; also the education and training of health professionals and the terms and conditions of service of NHS staff and general practitioners;

Education and training

- **school education** including pre-5, primary and secondary education, the functions of Her Majesty's Inspectorate of Schools and teacher supply, training and conditions of service;

- **further and higher education** including policy, funding, the functions of the Scottish Higher Education Funding Council (SHEFC) and student support;

- **science and research funding** where supported through SHEFC and where it is undertaken in support of other devolved matters;

- **training policy and lifelong learning** including all the training responsibilities presently exercised by The Scottish Office;

- **vocational qualifications** including the functions of the Scottish Qualifications Authority;

- **careers advice and guidance**;

Local government, social work and housing

- **local government** including local government finance and local domestic and non-domestic taxation;

- **social work** including the Children's Hearings system;

- **voluntary sector** issues;

- **housing** including the functions of Scottish Homes;

- **area regeneration** including the designation of enterprise zones;

- **land-use planning** and **building control**;

Economic development and transport

- **economic development** including the functions of Scottish Enterprise, Highlands and Islands Enterprise and the local enterprise companies;

- **financial assistance to industry** subject to common UK guidelines and consultation arrangements to be set out in a published concordat;

- **inward investment** including the functions of Locate in Scotland;

- promotion of **trade and exports** including the functions of Scottish Trade International;

- promotion of **tourism** including the functions of the Scottish Tourist Board;

- **passenger and road transport** covering the Scottish road network, the promotion of road safety, bus policy, concessionary fares, cycling, taxis and minicabs, non-technical aspects of disability and transport, some rail grant powers, the Strathclyde Passenger Transport Executive and consultative arrangements in respect of public transport;

- appropriate **air and sea transport** powers covering ports, harbours and piers, the provision of freight shipping and ferry services, the activities of Highlands and Islands Airports Ltd and planning and environmental issues relating to airports;

- **inland waterways**;

- **criminal law** and procedure except for offences created in statute law relating to reserved matters including drugs and firearms;

- **civil law** except in relation to matters which are reserved;

- **electoral law** in relation to local government elections;

- **judicial appointments** subject to the appointments of the Lord President of the Court of Session and the Lord Justice Clerk being made by The Queen on the advice of the Prime Minister on the basis of nominations from the Scottish Executive;

- the **criminal justice and prosecution** system;

- the **civil and criminal courts** including the functions of the Scottish Courts Administration and the Court of Lord Lyon;

- **tribunals** concerned with devolved matters and the Scottish Council on Tribunals;

- **legal aid**;

- **parole**, the release of life sentence prisoners and alleged miscarriages of justice;

- **prisons** including the functions of the Scottish Prison Service and the treatment of offenders;

- the **police and fire services** including fire safety;

- **civil defence** and **emergency planning**;

- functions under various **international legal agreements** in devolved areas, for example relating to child abduction and the reciprocal enforcement of Maintenance Orders;

- **liquor licensing;**

- **protection of animals** including protection against cruelty to domestic, captive and wild animals, zoo licensing, controlling dangerous wild animals and game;

Environment

- **the environment** including environmental protection, matters relating to air, land and water pollution and the functions of the Scottish Environment Protection Agency; water supplies and sewerage; and policies designed to promote sustainable development within the international commitments agreed by the UK;

- **the natural heritage** including countryside issues and the functions of Scottish Natural Heritage;

- the **built heritage** including the functions of Historic Scotland;

- **flood prevention, coast protection** and **reservoir safety**;

Agriculture, forestry and fishing

- **agriculture** including responsibility for implementing measures under the Common Agricultural Policy, and for domestic agriculture including crofting, animal and plant health and animal welfare subject to suitable co-ordination arrangements to ensure consistency within the UK where required under European law or to protect the public, animal or plant health or animal welfare;

- **food standards**: the relationship between the powers to be exercised by the Scottish Executive and the proposed Food Agency and the degree of UK co-ordination required to protect the public will be considered in the White Paper on the Agency to be issued in the autumn;

- **forestry**: the Secretary of State for Scotland's functions, including his power of direction over the Forestry Commission, will be transferred to the Scottish Executive, as will responsibility for finance for the Forestry Commission's activities in Scotland. The financial arrangements will be agreed on a fair and equitable basis taking into account the interests of UK tax payers in a suitable division of the receipts from the business activities of the Commission;

- **fisheries** including responsibility for implementing measures under the Common Fisheries Policy, subject to suitable co-ordination arrangements to ensure effective discharge of UK obligations; domestic fisheries matters including inshore sea fisheries, salmon and freshwater fisheries and aquaculture;

Sport and the arts

- **sport** including the activities of the Scottish Sports Council;

- **the arts** including the functions of the National Library of Scotland, the National Museums of Scotland, the National Galleries of Scotland, the Scottish Museums Council, the Scottish Arts Council, and Scottish Screen and support for Gaelic;

Other matters

- **statistics, public registers and records** including the responsibilities of the Keeper of the Registers, the Keeper of the Records, and the Registrar General for Scotland.

2.5　The Scottish Parliament will also be able to examine devolved matters and debate a wide range of issues of interest and concern in Scotland, whether devolved or reserved. The Scottish Parliament and Executive will be able to promote equal opportunities through policies and legislation in the full range of devolved matters. There will continue to be arrangements for the Scottish voice to be heard on UK-wide subjects such as women's issues.

The Scottish Executive

2.6　The Scottish Executive, which will be accountable to the Scottish Parliament, will exercise executive responsibility in relation to devolved matters. The relationship between the Scottish Executive and the Scottish Parliament will be similar to the relationship between the UK Government and the UK Parliament. The Executive will consist of the First Minister plus a team of Scottish Ministers including Law Officers. The statutory powers and duties exercised by Ministers of the Crown in Scotland in relation to devolved matters will be transferred to Ministers of the Scottish Executive.

2.7　In addition, the Scottish Executive will be responsible for certain administrative functions in areas where law-making powers will be reserved or are a matter for the EU. Most of these functions are already performed by the Secretary of State for Scotland. Transferring them to the Scottish Executive will allow detailed administrative arrangements to meet distinctive Scottish circumstances within a coherent and consistent UK legislative framework. Among the functions which the Scottish Executive will perform in this way will be: the administration in Scotland of the European Structural Funds; powers and duties in relation to electricity supply (including, for example, the granting of consent for the construction of a generating station or overhead electricity lines) and civil nuclear emergency planning; the determination of certain public sector pension schemes; an appropriate oversight role in relation to all Scottish passenger rail services; administration of freight facilities and track access grants; applications to the EU for the designation of lifeline air services; powers to issue policy and financial directions to National Lottery distributors in Scotland; designation of casino areas; and the setting of gaming hours and certain licence fees. The Executive will also be responsible for appointments of Justices of the Peace and General Commissioners of Income Tax; and some Crown, church and ceremonial matters.

Public bodies

2.8　The Parliament and its committees will hold public bodies exercising functions in relation to devolved matters to account for their actions in Scotland and will have the power to legislate in respect of these bodies.

2.9　The Scottish public bodies listed in Annex A will come within the remit of the Parliament. It will receive reports and will be able to investigate and monitor their activities; and it will be able to alter their structure or wind up existing bodies and create new ones. The Scottish Executive will inherit the existing powers of UK Ministers of the Crown to make appointments to, fund and direct the activities of these bodies.

2.10   In certain devolved areas where public bodies with a UK or GB remit presently operate it will be for the Scottish Parliament to decide whether to put in place separate Scottish bodies. The Government envisage however that the Scottish Parliament will want to continue most such UK or GB arrangements in the light of the advantages of sharing knowledge and expertise on a UK or GB basis and of the greater efficiency in the use of resources. The Scottish Parliament will have the power to require submission of reports and the presentation of oral evidence on the activities of such bodies and will be able to investigate, report on and debate what they do. Where UK/GB bodies are established on a statutory basis and have a remit which includes responsibility for devolved matters in Scotland, the Scottish Executive will have a statutory right to be consulted on their membership. There will also be a right to consultation on changes to terms of reference and on the exercise of any relevant statutory functions in respect of such bodies. There will be provision for transferring functions in respect of such bodies on a case by case basis to the Scottish Executive and for dealing with the practical consequences in the event that a body has to be split up. These provisions will apply to many bodies across the full range of devolved matters. Examples include: the UK Sports Council, the Central Council for Education and Training in Social Work, the Criminal Injuries Compensation Authority and the Meat Hygiene Service. There are also many non-statutory bodies with a UK or GB remit. In these cases arrangements based on these principles will be made under non-statutory agreements.

2.11   In certain reserved areas the activities of other UK/GB bodies which are accountable to the UK Parliament will continue to be significant in the economic or social life of Scotland, and therefore likely to be of interest to the Scottish Parliament. The Government propose that the Scottish Parliament should be able to invite the submission of reports and the presentation of oral evidence before its committees from bodies operating in reserved areas in relation to their activities in or affecting Scotland. Examples of such bodies are:

- energy regulators such as the Office of Electricity Regulation and the Office of Gas Supply;

- the Office of Passenger Rail Franchising and the Office of the Rail Regulator;

- the Health and Safety Commission;

- the Commission for Racial Equality and the Equal Opportunities Commission;

- the Employment Service and the Benefits Agency;

- broadcasting and telecommunication organisations such as the BBC and the Independent Television Commission[1] ;

- and the Post Office.

2.12 The Government believe that the powers they propose to devolve to the Scottish Parliament will enable it to bring renewed direction, confidence and prosperity to the people of Scotland; and improve the government of the United Kingdom.

---

1 The Scottish Executive will be consulted on the appointment of the National Governor of the BBC who represents Scottish interests, and on corresponding appointments to other broadcasting bodies.

CHAPTER 3

SCOTLAND WITHIN THE UNITED KINGDOM

3.1   The Government want a United Kingdom which everyone feels part of, can contribute to, and in whose future all have a stake. The Union will be strengthened by recognising the claims of Scotland, Wales and the regions with strong identities of their own. The Government's devolution proposals, by meeting these aspirations, will not only safeguard but also enhance the Union.

3.2   There are many matters which can be more effectively and beneficially handled on a United Kingdom basis. By preserving the integrity of the UK, the Union secures for its people participation in an economic unit which benefits business and provides access to wider markets and investment and increases prosperity for all. Scotland also benefits from strong and effective defence and foreign policies and a sense of belonging to a United Kingdom.

Reserved matters   3.3   The matters which the Government propose to reserve in the light of these considerations are listed below in general terms:

- **The constitution of the United Kingdom** including the Crown, the UK Parliament, electoral law, the Civil Service and the award of dignities and titles of honour;

- **UK foreign policy** including the ability to conclude European Union and other international agreements in both reserved and devolved areas and Ministry of International Development matters;

- **UK defence and national security** including responsibility for the armed forces and the security services, treason and other provisions for dealing with terrorism or subversion related to these matters;

- **The protection of borders and certain matters subject to border controls** including designation of the United Kingdom's land and maritime borders and fisheries limits, immigration and nationality, extradition, the criminal law in relation to drugs and firearms, and the regulation of drugs of misuse;

- **The stability of the UK's fiscal, economic and monetary system** including macroeconomic, monetary and fiscal affairs (except the tax varying and local taxation powers devolved under the Government's proposals), the granting of UK tax concessions and the currency;

- **Common markets for UK goods and services** at home and abroad including the law on companies and business associations, insurance, corporate insolvency and intellectual property, regulation of financial institutions and financial services, competition policy (subject to satisfactory rights of representation in the Scottish interest), consumer protection, regulation of the energy supply industries and international trade policy and Export Credit Guarantee Department matters;[1]

- **Employment legislation** including industrial relations, equal opportunities, health and safety and the matters for which the Employment Service is responsible;

- **Social security policy and administration**, including benefits and the matters for which the Benefits Agency is responsible, contributions, child support maintenance and occupational and personal pension regulation and related employment policy, services and assistance;

- **Regulation of certain professions** primarily where these are currently dealt with under UK statutes, including medical, dental, nursing and other health professions.[2] The Civil Service Commissioners, the UK Senior Salaries Review Body and primary legislation in respect of public service pensions will also be reserved matters;

- **Transport safety and regulation** including regulation of aviation and shipping, marine and air safety, rail safety and regulation (except for appropriate oversight by the Scottish Executive of Scottish passenger rail services), and some aspects of road traffic regulation.[3]

- **Certain other matters presently subject to UK or GB regulation or operation** including the UK Research Councils, nuclear safety, the control and safety of medicines, reciprocal health agreements, the designation of assisted areas, the Ordnance Survey, the regulatory framework for broadcasting and film classification including the regulation of the distribution of video recordings, the licensing of theatres and cinemas, cultural property matters dealt with at UK level, gambling and the National Lottery and data protection. In addition a number of matters in the health sector, including abortion, human fertilisation and embryology, genetics, xenotransplantation and vivisection will be reserved in view of the need for a common approach. Equality legislation (covering racial, gender and disability discrimination) will be reserved.

3.4   The Government believe that reserving powers in these areas will safeguard the integrity of the UK and the benefits of a consistent and integrated approach.

---

1 Reserved matters under this heading also include wireless telegraphy and telecommunications regulation and licensing, the regulation of pharmaceutical prices, postal services, weights and measures and technical standards of goods and the regulation of time zones.

2 Professions outside the health sector the regulation of which will be reserved will include veterinary surgeons, architects, auditors, estate agents, insolvency practitioners and insurance intermediaries.

3 Other transport matters to be reserved include transport security, driver and vehicle licensing and testing, road haulage, vehicle standards, general speed limits, marine, air and rail accident prevention and investigation, some other aspects of road safety and road traffic regulation and technical standards relating to transport of disabled persons.

CHAPTER 4

THE NEW CONSTITUTIONAL ARRANGEMENTS

4.1   This Chapter has four key elements: the nature of the constitutional arrangements; the structure of Scottish government; the future liaison machinery between Edinburgh and Westminster; and mechanisms for reaching agreement on any contested issue of competence.

Nature of the new constitutional arrangements

4.2   Under the Government's proposals, the UK Parliament will devolve wide ranging legislative powers to the Scottish Parliament. Scotland will of course remain an integral part of the United Kingdom. The Queen will continue to be Head of State of the United Kingdom. The UK Parliament is and will remain sovereign in all matters: but as part of the Government's resolve to modernise the British constitution Westminster will be choosing to exercise that sovereignty by devolving legislative responsibilities to a Scottish Parliament without in any way diminishing its own powers. The Government recognise that no UK Parliament can bind its successors. The Government however believe that the popular support for the Scottish Parliament, once established, will make sure that its future in the UK constitution will be secure.

4.3   The Government have given careful thought to the best way of building stability into the settlement. The Scotland Act 1978 provided for the transfer of specified areas of legislative and executive competence, as set out in Schedules 10 and 11 to the Act. It would have required frequent updating and might have given rise to regular legal arguments about whether particular matters were or were not devolved. This approach now seems incompatible with the Government's objective of ensuring maximum clarity and stability. Consequently the legislation establishing the Scottish Parliament will follow the approach of the Northern Ireland Constitution Act 1973 in listing matters reserved to the UK Parliament rather than specifying devolved matters.

4.4   There will be provision for transferring further matters to and from the reserved list by Order in Council, which would be approved by both Parliaments. This will enable the boundary between reserved and devolved matters to be adjusted as appropriate and as the need arises. There may be instances (e.g. international obligations which touch on devolved as well as reserved matters) where it will be more convenient for legislation to be passed by the UK Parliament.

4.5   Scotland's Members of Parliament will continue to play a full and constructive part in the proceedings of the House of Commons. This is right both for Scotland

and the United Kingdom because devolution is about strengthening the United Kingdom. The distribution of seats in the House of Commons will be reviewed by the Parliamentary Boundary Commissions which follow criteria defined in statute. At present, special statutory provisions stipulate a minimum number of Scottish seats. The Government have decided that in the next review this requirement will no longer apply. Other statutory requirements, notably the need to give due weight to geographical considerations and local ties, will continue to apply to reviews for Scotland in the same way as they will apply to reviews for other parts of the UK.

4.6   It will be for the House of Commons to consider its future arrangements for Scottish business.

The structure of government in Scotland

4.7   As outlined in Chapter 2, executive power in devolved areas will be exercised by the Scottish Executive. The Scottish Parliament will hold the Executive to account for its actions. Ministers of the Scottish Executive will be answerable to the Scottish Parliament, and that Parliament's committees will be able to scrutinise and report on the effectiveness of the Executive's administrative action and its use of public monies voted to it by the Parliament.

4.8   The Scottish Executive will require the services of Law Officers to provide it with advice on legal matters and to represent its interests in the courts. The responsibilities of the Lord Advocate for the prosecution and investigation of crimes and offences (including those relating to reserved matters) are to be devolved. It is therefore appropriate that the Law Officers of the Scottish Executive should be the Lord Advocate and the Solicitor General for Scotland. The traditional independence of the Lord Advocate as public prosecutor will be maintained.

4.9   The UK Government will continue to need advice on Scots law (whether reserved or devolved). Accordingly a new post of Scottish Law Officer to the United Kingdom Government will be created.

4.10   As noted in Chapter 1, the Government are committed to Freedom of Information legislation throughout the UK. The Scottish Parliament will be able to determine the approach of the Scottish Executive and other Scottish public bodies to openness and the freedom of information within areas of devolved competence.

4.11   In the UK context, the Parliamentary Commissioner for Administration (often known as the Parliamentary Ombudsman) is independently appointed to investigate complaints about the Government's handling of matters. He will continue to deal with complaints from Scotland about the UK Government's handling of matters where responsibility has not been devolved. For complaints about the handling of devolved matters, there will be similar arrangements for Scotland, based as closely as possible on the UK Ombudsman legislation.

4.12 The role of the Secretary of State for Scotland will be to secure the passage and implementation of the legislation to establish the Scottish Parliament; and then to support its initial development. Once the Scottish Parliament is in being, and the Scottish Executive established, the responsibilities of the Secretary of State for Scotland will change. The focus will be on promoting communication between the Scottish Parliament and Executive and between the UK Parliament and Government on matters of mutual interest; and on representing Scottish interests in reserved areas.

4.13 The Scottish Executive will need to keep in close touch with Departments of the UK Government. Good communication systems will be vital. Departments in both administrations will develop mutual understandings covering the appropriate exchange of information, advance notification and joint working. The principles will be as follows:

- the vast majority of matters should be capable of being handled routinely among officials of the Departments in question;

- if further discussion is needed on any issue, the Cabinet Office and its Scottish Executive counterpart will mediate, again at official level;

- on some issues there will need to be discussions between the Scottish Executive and Ministers in the UK Government.

4.14 Representatives of the UK Government (usually the Secretary of State for Scotland) and the Scottish Executive will meet from time to time, to discuss particular issues or simply to take stock of relations. These arrangements will be updated regularly to reflect the evolution of administrative conventions of co-operation and joint working.

4.15 The Scottish Executive and the UK Government may from time to time take different views of the Scottish Parliament's legislative powers. There will therefore be procedures for identifying and resolving any such difficulties. The Government believe that, given an open and constructive relationship between the UK Government and the Scottish Executive, problems will usually be resolved quickly and amicably.

4.16 In drafting legislation for consideration by the Scottish Parliament, the Scottish Executive will take legal advice to ensure that the provisions brought forward are within the Scottish Parliament's powers. In any cases of uncertainty, there will be consultation with the Scottish Executive Law Officers and as necessary more widely. It will be for the Presiding Officer of the Scottish Parliament to satisfy himself or herself that legislation, whether brought forward by the Executive or by others, is intra vires before giving approval to introduction. These pre-legislative checks will ensure that any potential difficulties are identified at the earliest possible point. During the Parliamentary passage of legislation, it will fall to the Presiding Officer to certify that all amendments selected for debate are within the remit of the Scottish Parliament. UK Government Departments will be able to discuss any concerns which they might have with the Scottish Executive at that stage.

4.17   Prior to a Scottish Bill being passed forward from the Presiding Officer to receive Royal Assent, there will be a short delay period to ensure that the UK Government is content as to vires. In the event of a dispute between the Scottish Executive and the UK Government about vires remaining unresolved, there will be provision for it to be referred to the Judicial Committee of the Privy Council. For this purpose the Judicial Committee will consist of the Lords of Appeal in Ordinary. At least five Law Lords will sit in any case. The size and composition of the Committee will be decided by the Senior Law Lord (or, in his absence, the next senior Law Lord who is available) who will also decide where the Committee is to sit in any particular case. As appropriate, this might be in Edinburgh. The Judicial Committee will also be able to hear any subsequent disputes about devolution issues in relation to secondary legislation and Acts of the Scottish Parliament after Royal Assent.

International relations

4.18   Special arrangements will be needed for the handling of questions of international relations, and for the exercise of domestic powers which are capable of affecting the UK's international relations. The guiding principle is that the UK should be able to speak with one voice in the international arena and to advance policies (for example in international negotiations) which take proper account of the interests of all parts of the UK. It will also be essential that the UK Government is in a position to implement obligations it has undertaken in good faith internationally or which are imposed on the United Kingdom by international law.

4.19   For these principles to be implemented effectively where devolved areas of responsibility are involved, arrangements will be made for the Scottish Executive to play a part in the conduct of international negotiations through close liaison with the Whitehall Departments concerned; or in appropriate cases through direct representation on the UK delegation. The Scottish Executive and Parliament will also, where necessary, implement the international obligations which fall on the UK Government and Parliament.

4.20   The implications for devolution of incorporating the European Convention on Human Rights into domestic law will be dealt with as part of the process of legislating for incorporation. The Government will be setting out their proposals for this in a White Paper to be published later this year.

4.21   In summary, the proposals set out in this Chapter establish a clear and durable framework within which the Scottish Parliament and Scottish Executive can exercise their powers and discharge their responsibilities. The detailed settlement set out above will provide a firm foundation for future relationships.

CHAPTER 5

RELATIONS WITH THE EUROPEAN UNION

5.1   Relations with Europe are the responsibility of the United Kingdom Parliament and Government. But the Scottish Parliament and Executive will have an important role in those aspects of European Union business which affect devolved areas. This Chapter sets out arrangements to give effect to that role.

5.2   The Government are already demonstrating that the UK can pursue a more active and constructive approach to the European Union. We are also taking steps to ensure that the role of The Scottish Office, as part of the UK Government, is fully realised. UK Departments necessarily have the lead role in EU matters. Within this context, the Government are promoting full involvement of Scottish Office Ministers in EU Councils. This builds on their membership of relevant Cabinet and Cabinet Committees and the full involvement of Scottish Office officials in discussions with their Whitehall colleagues, and with the UK Permanent Representation (UKREP), the European Commission and others when EU matters relevant to Scotland are being considered. The setting up of a Scottish Parliament provides new opportunities for Scotland to make its important contribution to the UK's enhanced role.

5.3   The people of Scotland will continue to benefit from the influence which the UK has as a major member state within the European Union. By drawing on the contribution of the Scottish Executive, the UK will share an advantage already enjoyed by other member states with a tier of regional government. The existence of clear and distinctive domestic voices from regional government is already a source of strength for other member states. The Government will learn from best practice in those member states with strong regional government and adapt it to the needs of Scotland and the UK.

Policy formation and negotiation

5.4   EU policies and legislation will have a considerable effect on many of the matters for which the Scottish Parliament will be responsible. The UK Government wishes to involve the Scottish Executive as directly and as fully as possible in the Government's decision making on EU matters. It is part of the Government's intention that Scottish Executive Ministers and officials should be fully involved in discussions within the UK Government about the formulation of the UK's policy position on all issues which touch on devolved matters. This will require, of course, mutual respect for the confidentiality of those discussions and adherence to the resultant UK line, without which it would be impossible to maintain such close working relationships.

5.5   Our proposals are designed to give the Scottish Parliament and Scottish Executive the opportunity to work constructively for the common interests of Scotland and the UK. The success of such a close working relationship, and the ability to sustain it, will depend upon the way in which the Scottish Parliament and Executive respond to that opportunity.

5.6   The Government also propose that Ministers and officials of the Scottish Executive should have a role to play in relevant Council meetings and other negotiations with our EU partners. Policy does not remain static in negotiations; and continuing involvement is a necessary extension of involvement in formulating the UK's initial policy positions. The role of Scottish Ministers and officials will be to support and advance the single UK negotiating line which they have played a part in developing. The emphasis in negotiations has to be on working as a UK team; and the UK lead Minister will retain overall responsibility for the negotiations and determine how best each member of the team can contribute to securing the agreed policy position, so that, in appropriate cases, Scottish Executive Ministers could speak for the UK in Councils. They would do so with the full weight of the UK's status as a large member state behind them, because the policy positions advanced will have been agreed among the UK interests.

Scrutiny and implementation of EU legislation

5.7   The Scottish Parliament will be able to scrutinise EU legislative proposals to ensure that Scotland's interests are properly reflected. The UK Government will take into account the views of the Scottish Parliament and the UK Parliament may also wish to do so in its scrutiny processes. This requires, of course, that the Scottish Parliament's views are available early enough to enable this to happen. The Scottish Parliament and Executive will be able to determine how best to organise the scrutiny process to make it as effective as possible.

5.8   The Scottish Executive will have an obligation to ensure the implementation in Scotland of EU obligations which concern devolved matters. This will include the option of agreeing to GB or UK legislation, if it judges it appropriate. It is implicit in the sovereignty of the UK Parliament that it will continue to have the ability to legislate to give effect to EU obligations in Scotland. The Scottish Executive will be directly accountable through the Scottish courts to anyone affected by shortcomings in its implementation or enforcement of EU obligations. Where EU obligations are to be implemented separately for Scotland, there will be arrangements with the UK Government to ensure that differences of approach are compatible with the need for consistency of effect; and to avoid the risk of financial penalties falling on the UK for any failure of implementation or enforcement. If any such financial penalties were imposed on the UK, or penalties arose from infraction proceedings, responsibility for meeting them would have to be borne by the Scottish Executive if it were responsible for the failure; and the same principle would apply to the other parts of the UK.

Links with European institutions

5.9   Influence within the EU begins well before the process of formal negotiations between member states; and operates through many more channels than the formal Community, and inter-governmental processes. Scotland will be able to play its part in the less formal discussions with the institutions of the EU and interests within other member states. Scotland is already represented by its MEPs and its members of the Committee of the Regions and the Economic and Social Committee. The Scottish Executive will be responsible for making proposals to the Scottish Parliament on nominations to Scotland's established share of representation within the Committee of the Regions and the Economic and Social Committee; and it will be consulted by the UK Government on appointments to other European Institutions, where appropriate.

5.10   It is the norm for regional governments within the EU to have representative offices in Brussels. The Scottish Executive may well consider that such an office would assist Scotland's direct relationships with regional governments and with institutions in Brussels. It would complement rather than cut across the work of UKREP, which will remain responsible for representing the views of the United Kingdom to the European Institutions;   and provide an effective channel of communication with the Scottish Executive. This would be a separate role from that which Scotland Europa currently fulfils for its broad membership of private and public sector bodies, from Scotland and elsewhere.

5.11   UKREP plays a vital role in representing The Scottish Office's interests, along with those of the rest of the UK. Scottish Office staff have been seconded regularly to UKREP and that will continue to be the case for staff of the Scottish Executive. The secondment of civil servants and others from Scotland to serve in the Institutions of the European Community will also continue.

5.12   The guiding principle which the UK Government sets out to establish in the relationship with the Scottish Executive on EU matters is that there should be the closest possible working relationships and involvement. Provided the Scottish Executive is willing to work in that spirit of collaboration and trust, there will be an integrated process which builds upon the benefits of the current role of The Scottish Office within government. Taken together these arrangements will allow Scotland, within the UK, to develop its role in the European Union.

CHAPTER 6

RELATIONS WITH LOCAL GOVERNMENT AND OTHER BODIES

6.1   This Chapter sets out how the Scottish Parliament and Scottish Executive will relate to local government and other public bodies in the new Scotland. Local government, representing as it does communities throughout Scotland, is of particular importance. There is also a range of public bodies listed in Annex A which have a significant role in Scotland's life; these include the National Health Service in Scotland and other health bodies.

General principles   6.2   In establishing a Scottish Parliament to extend democratic accountability, the Government do not expect the Scottish Parliament and its Executive to accumulate a range of new functions at the centre which would be more appropriately and efficiently delivered by other bodies within Scotland. The Government believe that the principle that decisions should be made as close as possible to the citizen holds good within Scotland as it does within the United Kingdom.

6.3   The Government believe that the new arrangements should be based on the following principles:

- the Scottish Parliament should set the national framework within which other Scottish public bodies operate;

- local authorities, NDPBs and other Scottish public bodies should be open and accountable to the Scottish people either through the Scottish Parliament and its Executive or in the case of local authorities directly through local elections.

6.4   The establishment of a Scottish Parliament will provide an opportunity to re-examine the roles and responsibilities of some of these bodies. The Government recognise that the relationship between the Scottish Parliament and Scottish Executive and local authorities is particularly crucial to the good governance of Scotland and the effective provision of services to its people. That is why the Government will shortly establish an independent committee to study how to build the most effective relations between the Scottish Parliament and Scottish Executive and a strong and effective local government. The committee's report will be laid before the Scottish Parliament.

Local government   6.5   The Scottish Parliament will have general responsibility for legislation and policy relating to local government. The Scottish Parliament will have the power to set the framework within which local government operates and to legislate to make changes to the powers, boundaries and functions of local authorities. The Scottish Executive will be responsible for supporting local authority current expenditure and for controlling and allocating capital allocations to Scottish councils. It will also be responsible for the system of local taxation.

6.6   The Government believe the Scottish people will be served best by a Scottish Parliament and Scottish Executive working closely with strong democratically elected local government. The Government demonstrated their commitment to local government by signing the Council of Europe Charter of Local Self-Government on 3 June, only a month after coming into office. It will be for the Scottish Parliament and its Executive to determine the details of their relationships with local authorities and funding and taxation arrangements for local government in the light of developments between now and the establishment of the Scottish Parliament, and the recommendations of the independent committee.

Public bodies

6.7   The Government recognise that some executive functions of government are best delivered by public bodies established for the purpose provided that democratic accountability is ultimately retained by Ministers. However the Government are concerned at the extent to which Scotland's vital public services are now run by unelected bodies.

6.8   The Scottish Executive will have responsibility for all Scottish public bodies whose functions and services will be devolved, and will be accountable to the Scottish Parliament for them. The Scottish Executive will assume the responsibilities of Ministers of the Crown in relation to these bodies. The Scottish Executive will be required to put arrangements in place to ensure that appointments to Scottish public bodies are subject to independent scrutiny and conform to the Commissioner of Public Appointments' Code of Practice.

Health bodies

6.9   The Scottish Parliament will be responsible for ensuring that the needs and priorities of Scotland are reflected in the development of the National Health Service in Scotland. It will be for the Scottish Parliament to decide the details of its relationship with health bodies, including funding arrangements.

6.10   Overall, the Government intend that relationships between the Scottish Parliament and its Executive and local government and other public bodies should be complementary, with the emphasis on solutions which give the best possible service and value for money to the people of Scotland. The Government wish to leave detailed arrangements for the Scottish Parliament and its Executive to develop for themselves.

CHAPTER 7

FINANCIAL ARRANGEMENTS

7.1   This Chapter discusses the financial arrangements which will apply to the Scottish Parliament. It proposes a continuation of the existing "Block and formula" system of funding most of Scotland's public expenditure programmes which has applied continuously since the late 1970s.   There will of course be adjustments to reflect the terms of the financial arrangements arising out of the Bill which will follow this White Paper.   It proposes also that the Scottish Parliament should be able to raise limited income at its own hand by means of a defined but limited power to vary income tax in Scotland and that the Scottish Parliament should be responsible for local government finance including local taxation.

Objectives

7.2   The financial arrangements for the Scottish Parliament will be designed to ensure that:

- Scotland will continue to benefit from its appropriate share of UK public expenditure;

- the Scottish Parliament's assigned budget is determined by a method which is objective, transparent and widely accepted;

- the Scottish Parliament has the maximum freedom to determine its own expenditure priorities;

- the Scottish Parliament has a defined and limited power to vary central government taxation in Scotland and alter its overall spending accordingly;

- the UK Government can maintain proper control over public expenditure and public borrowing at the UK level;

- there are clear lines of accountability for local government spending and taxation; and

- UK taxpayers as a whole will be insulated from the effects of local decisions which add to Exchequer-funded expenditure in Scotland.

Present arrangements

7.3   For many years most of the expenditure programmes which fall within the Secretary of State for Scotland's budget have been controlled through an arrangement known commonly as the Scottish Block.   Under this arrangement a block of resources, the annual changes in which have been determined by means of a population-based formula, has been made available annually to the Secretary of State for Scotland, who has then had the freedom to distribute those resources between Scottish programmes as he has thought fit. He has not been bound to replicate the spending decisions of Whitehall Departments but has been able annually to determine a specific Scottish set of priorities. Annex B provides further details of how the Block currently operates and how it will do so under the new arrangements.

7.4 In practice these arrangements, based on the Block and formula, have produced fair settlements for Scotland in annual public expenditure rounds and have allowed the Secretary of State for Scotland to determine his spending decisions in accordance with Scottish needs and priorities. They have largely removed the need for annual negotiation between The Scottish Office and the Treasury. The Government have therefore concluded that the financial framework for the Scottish Parliament should be based on these existing arrangements with, in future, the Scottish Parliament determining Scottish spending priorities.

The assigned budget

7.5 The Scottish Parliament will have an overall assigned budget broadly comparable to the present overall budget of the Secretary of State for Scotland. The majority of the assigned budget will be a new Block and, subject to paragraph 7.7 below, any future changes to the Block will be determined through the formula-based arrangements which have become known as the "Barnett formula". The details of the operation of the formula each year will be a matter of public record.

7.6 In practice, therefore, the Scottish Parliament's assigned budget, like the Secretary of State's budget at present, will be determined each year largely through the Block arrangements. The annual changes to the new Block will be calculated by reference to the existing formula, providing continuity with current arrangements. That means that each year the new Block will be adjusted by the population share of changes to comparable English or English and Welsh programmes.

7.7 The formula will be updated from time to time to take account of population and other technical changes. Any more substantial revision would need to be preceded by an in depth study of relative spending requirements and would be the subject of full consultation between the Scottish Executive and the UK Government.

7.8 Once the amount of the assigned budget for any forthcoming year is determined the Scottish Executive, subject to the consent of the Scottish Parliament and to its legal obligations, will have complete freedom to allocate resources across the programmes within the assigned budget.

7.9 Decisions taken by the Scottish Parliament or Executive will sometimes have financial implications for Departments of the UK Government. Similarly, UK Government Departments may on occasion implement policies which will lead to additional costs for the Scottish Parliament. Generally, it will be right, in line with long-standing conventions, for the body whose decision leads to higher or extra costs to meet those costs. This general rule will continue to apply between the Scottish Parliament and Executive and UK Government Departments. Many of the UK Government's decisions will result in automatic adjustments for Scotland through the Barnett formula.

Funding

7.10   Once the proportion of the assigned budget which requires Exchequer funding has been determined, the UK Parliament will be invited to vote the necessary resources through a grant.   Further elements of the assigned budget will be covered, as at present, by funding from the European Union and by borrowing by local authorities and other public bodies, to fund their capital spending. The Scottish Parliament will have power to authorise the Scottish Executive to undertake short-term borrowing to assist in the short-term matching of income and expenditure.   It will not have a long-term borrowing power on its own account.

Tax varying powers

7.11   Subject to the outcome of the proposed referendum on this issue the Scottish Parliament will be given a power to vary tax.

7.12   The Government propose that the tax varying power should operate on income tax, because it is broadly based and easy to administer.   Income tax is relatively simple and easy to understand and has none of the difficulties associated with the other major tax bases: different rates of VAT on different sides of the border would cause practical problems and there would be specific difficulties with EU rules;   corporation tax would place an unreasonable burden on companies operating in Scotland;   National Insurance is inappropriate because of its direct link with the social security system; and council tax and non-domestic rates would over-burden the local government finance system and undermine the accountability of local government to its electorate.

7.13   The Scottish Parliament will have the power to increase or decrease the basic rate of income tax set by the UK Parliament by a maximum of 3p.   This is consistent with the recommendations of the Scottish Constitutional Convention.   Since each 1p change would currently vary revenue by around £150m, the Scottish Parliament would be able to levy or to reduce income tax for basic rate taxpayers in Scotland by up to around £450m.   It is of course possible that future changes to the UK income tax structure might reduce the value of the product of the Scottish Parliament's tax-varying power.   In these circumstances, the Parliament's ability to raise or forgo up to £450m through the tax system will be preserved.   This sum will be index linked to maintain its real value.

7.14   Any mechanism that might be required in future for protecting the Scottish tax take would be dependent upon the tax structure that was in place or had been announced at that time. As the Scottish Parliament will be fully operational from the financial year 2000-01 onwards, the appropriate arrangements would have to be jointly discussed by the Scottish Executive and the UK Government as and when such circumstances arose.

7.15   Savings and dividend income under current arrangements will not be subject to the Scottish Parliament's 3p basic rate power as it is taxed only at the lower or higher rate.   The Government believe that savings and dividend income should in future remain exempt from any income tax variation power, in order to ensure that such income is taxed on a consistent basis throughout the UK, thus avoiding economic distortion.

7.16   The test of liability will be residence - a well established concept in tax law. A Scottish resident will be an individual who is resident in the UK for income tax purposes and who in any tax year either spends at least half of his time in Scotland (when in the UK) or whose principal home is in Scotland.   These concepts will be set out in legislation.

7.17   Any tax due to the Scottish Parliament will be collected by the Inland Revenue. Normal arrangements would apply. Self-employed taxpayers would pay through their Self Assessment. Employees would pay through PAYE with their employers operating a special tax table which would reflect any varied rate set by the Scottish Parliament.

7.18   The direct costs to the Government of establishing the mechanisms for tax variation in Scotland is estimated at around £10m. Running costs for the Government of collecting the tax are expected to be around £8m per annum, but may vary depending upon whether or not the Scottish Parliament chooses to vary the rate of tax. The Scottish Parliament will meet the administration costs incurred by the Inland Revenue.

7.19   Collection through PAYE will also generate additional costs for employers. Their setting up costs are estimated to be around £50m (which could be phased) and running costs at around £6-£15m. Costs will vary from employer to employer. For illustrative purposes, an employer with 5 Scottish resident employees, (most cases in practice) would typically face setting-up costs in the range £50-£100. A larger firm, with 200 Scottish resident employees operating PAYE could expect set up costs in the range of £700-£1,400, around £5 per employee. Once the legislation enacting the tax-varying power is in place, the Government will publish a formal compliance cost assessment, following consultation with employers.

7.20   If the Scottish Parliament exercises the tax-varying powers the resources available to it will be adjusted upwards or downwards by the appropriate amount.

Local government expenditure

7.21   The case for the Scottish Parliament is built on the range of powers and legislative responsibilities which it will enjoy. It follows that the Scottish Parliament's control of the powers and functions of Scottish local government should extend to the financing of local government expenditure. This represents continuity with long established arrangements.

7.22   The Government's objective is to establish clear lines of accountability for local government spending and taxation. Its aim is a system in which fiscal self-discipline is reinforced, both by the proper accountability of local authorities and the Scottish Parliament to their respective electorates and by the obligation on the Scottish Parliament to absorb any costs for UK taxpayers flowing from decisions on local government finance.

7.23 Support for local authority current expenditure will remain in the new Block, and so will capital allocations to councils. Responsibility for the control of local authority spending - current and capital - will be a devolved matter, so that the Scottish Parliament will have discretion to alter the existing regimes if it wishes, provided of course it stays within the total of the assigned budget. Local authorities will continue to be able to borrow from the Public Works Loan Board under existing arrangements.

7.24 The remainder of local authority self-financed expenditure, which consists largely of council tax revenue will, as at present, fall outwith the Scottish Parliament's assigned budget just as, at present, it falls outside the Scottish Block. The Scottish Parliament will have the powers to control local authority current expenditure, through capping or other means, and it will be for the Scottish Parliament to decide whether and how to exercise these powers. Should self-financed expenditure start to rise steeply, the Scottish Parliament would clearly come under pressure from council tax payers in Scotland to exercise its powers. If growth relative to England were excessive and were such as to threaten targets set for public expenditure as part of the management of the UK economy, and the Scottish Parliament nevertheless chose not to exercise its powers, it would be open to the UK Government to take the excess into account in considering the level of their support for expenditure in Scotland.

7.25 Decisions by local authorities on their council tax levels and their housing rent levels could lead to expenditure on council tax benefits and rent rebates growing more rapidly in Scotland than in England. This could put an unfair burden on UK taxpayers. Arrangements will therefore be made to include the resources for these benefits in the Block, so that any resultant extra costs would have to be found by the Scottish Parliament.

Local taxation 7.26 The Scottish Parliament will be responsible for determining the form of local taxation, both domestic and non-domestic, which local authorities will be permitted to levy. It will therefore be able to alter the form of the council tax, or replace it if it so decides. Non-domestic rates are also an important part of the local finance system, and they too will be a devolved matter. It will be for the Scottish Parliament to decide whether to retain the power to set the non-domestic rate poundage within its own control or to devolve that responsibility to local councils. It will clearly need to consult business interests before making any changes. In the period until the Scottish Parliament is established, the Government will continue with their existing policy for non-domestic rates.

Propriety and
value for money

7.27   The detailed arrangements which the Scottish Parliament makes to control and scrutinise the spending of the Scottish Executive will be a matter for the Scottish Parliament and its committees, but the Scotland Bill will lay a general obligation on the Scottish Parliament to establish effective scrutiny and audit arrangements. Suitable machinery will have to be agreed before the Scottish Parliament becomes fully operational to ensure that the actions of the Scottish Executive can be called to account as soon as it assumes its responsibilities. In common with other central government expenditure the grant to the Scottish Parliament will fall to be audited by the UK Comptroller and Auditor General.

7.28   These arrangements provide a structure for funding the Scottish Parliament that will establish that Parliament on a sound financial basis both on its own terms and in terms of its relationship with the rest of the UK. The system will provide an important element of continuity and the stability necessary for sensible long-term planning. It crucially will introduce direct accountability for spending priorities in Scotland.   The proposals provide new opportunities.   They will support the establishment of a powerful and effective Scottish Parliament capable of serving fully Scotland's interests and at the same time they recognise and acknowledge the continuing and legitimate interests of the UK as a whole.

CHAPTER 8

ELECTORAL ARRANGEMENTS

8.1   The Government believe that electoral arrangements for the Scottish Parliament should reflect the will of the Scottish people. A constituency link will be the essential foundation of the new Scottish Parliament. However it is also important to provide for greater proportionality to build stability into the overall settlement. It is therefore proposed that there be a significant number of additional Members elected on a wider and proportional basis, in order to bring a closer relationship between votes cast and seats won. This Chapter sets out who will be able to vote, who will be able to stand, and how the electoral system will work.

Constituencies   8.2   Members will be known as Members of the Scottish Parliament (MSPs). They will be elected in two different ways. The majority will be elected from constituencies which are the same as the constituencies of the Westminster Parliament except that Orkney and Shetland (which at the moment form one constituency) will become 2 separate constituencies thus making 73 in total. The remaining 56 Members - "additional Members" - will be selected from party lists drawn up for each of the current European Parliament constituencies. There will be 7 additional Members from each constituency.

Electoral register   8.3   The electoral register for elections to the Scottish Parliament will be based on residency, and will be the same as for local government elections. This means that Members of the House of Lords resident in Scotland and EC nationals resident in Scotland will be able to vote. Commonwealth citizens and citizens of the Republic of Ireland resident in Scotland will also be included. The register will however exclude overseas electors i.e. those who have taken up residence outside the UK but who have been registered on an electoral register in Scotland at some point during the previous 20 years.

Eligibility to stand   8.4   Those eligible to stand for the Scottish Parliament will be UK citizens, including Peers, Peeresses in their own right, Priests and Ministers of religion. Commonwealth citizens and Republic of Ireland citizens will also be able to stand as will EU citizens resident in the UK. Otherwise, broadly the same disqualifications as for the House of Commons will apply. All will have to be 21 or over.

8.5   The Government are keen to see people with standing in their communities and who represent the widest possible range of interests in Scotland putting themselves forward for election to the Scottish Parliament. In particular the Government attach great importance to equal opportunities for all - including women, members of ethnic minorities and disabled people. The Government urge all political parties offering candidates for election to the Scottish Parliament to have this in mind in their internal candidate selection processes.

Electoral system   8.6   Annex C sets out in more detail how the electoral system will work.

Changes in electoral arrangements   8.7   The integrity of the UK will be strengthened by common UK and Scottish Parliament boundaries. Responsibility for Scottish Parliamentary electoral arrangements and constituencies will be reserved matters; the Parliamentary Boundary Commission for Scotland will continue in being, and future changes in electoral arrangements for the Scottish Parliament will therefore be a matter for the UK Parliament, subject to consultation with the Scottish Parliament. Any changes in Westminister constituencies will result in changes to Scottish Parliamentary constituencies; and may also lead to consequential adjustments to the size of the Scottish Parliament so as to maintain the present balance between constituency and additional Member seats.

8.8   Taken together, the electoral arrangements set out above will secure for Scotland a Parliament built on fairness.

CHAPTER 9

PARLIAMENTARY ARRANGEMENTS

9.1   The Government intend the minimum of legislation to establish the Scottish Parliament; and wherever possible to leave the Scottish Parliament to decide for itself what its procedures should be. This Chapter sets out the basic constitutional arrangements which the Government will put in place, within which the Scottish Parliament will operate according to its own procedures.

MSPs

9.2   Members of the Scottish Parliament will be elected for a fixed term of 4 years. The legislation will not prohibit dual mandates (i.e. an MSP being also a member of the UK or European Parliaments or a local authority councillor). This will be a matter for individual political parties.

9.3   The Government will invite the independent Senior Salaries Review Body to set the salaries of MSPs in the first instance. Thereafter the Government will expect movements to be linked to changes in the salaries received by MPs. It will be for the Scottish Parliament to determine the allowances to be paid to MSPs.

9.4   The Scottish Parliament may be dissolved before the 4 years is up with the agreement of at least two thirds of MSPs, or if the Parliament fails to agree on the appointment of a First Minister.

9.5   A Presiding Officer and two deputies will be elected from amongst Members by a vote of the full Scottish Parliament. The Presiding Officer will ensure the efficient conduct and administration of Scottish Parliamentary business and chair sessions of that Parliament.

Ministers

9.6   The First Minister will head the Scottish Executive and will be appointed by The Queen on the advice of the Presiding Officer after the Scottish Parliament has nominated a candidate, who will normally be the leader of the party able to command the majority support of the Scottish Parliament. The First Minister will (with the approval of The Queen) appoint other Ministers; and will determine portfolios.

9.7   The Scottish Law Officers will be appointed by Royal Warrant. The Scottish Law Officers need not be MSPs: if not MSPs, they will be entitled to attend and speak, but not vote, in proceedings of the Scottish Parliament and its committees.

How the Scottish Parliament will work

9.8   The Scottish Parliament will be responsible for drawing up and adopting Standing Orders. The Government intend that these Standing Orders be designed to ensure openness, responsiveness and accountability. There will be minimum requirements covering stages of Bills, Crown interests, preservation of order, Members' pecuniary interests, reporting of proceedings, public access and committees.

9.9   The Government wish so far as possible to leave detailed decisions on how the Scottish Parliament will work to that Parliament itself. The Government expect that the Scottish Parliament will adopt modern methods of working; that it will be accessible, open and responsive to the needs of the public; that participation by organisations and individuals in decision making will be encouraged; and that views and advice from specialists will be sought as appropriate.

9.10   The Government also expect committees to play an important part in carrying out Parliamentary business and the Scottish Parliament will have power to establish such committees as it considers appropriate. It is envisaged that these committees might for example initiate legislation, scrutinise and amend the Scottish Executive's proposals as well as having wide-ranging investigative functions. Such a role for the Scottish Parliament committees will mean that the proposals of the Scottish Executive will be appropriately scrutinised. The committees might meet from time to time at appropriate locations throughout Scotland so that people can see how their country is run.

9.11   In summary, the Government will provide a framework for the Scottish Parliament, but it will be left open to that Parliament itself to develop procedures which best meet its purposes.

CHAPTER 10

MAKING IT HAPPEN

10.1   This Chapter sets out the steps to be taken to service and support the Scottish Parliament and the Scottish Executive and outlines the associated capital and running costs.

A home fit for the Scottish Parliament

10.2   The building the Scottish Parliament occupies must be of such a quality, durability and civic importance as to reflect the Parliament's status and operational needs; it must be secure but also accessible to all including people with special needs; it must promote modern and efficient ways of working and good environmental practice.

10.3   It will be an important symbol for Scotland. It should pay tribute to the country's past achievements and signal its future aspirations. It must be flexible enough to accommodate changes over time in operational requirements. Quality and value for money are also key considerations.

10.4   The accommodation must allow Scottish Parliamentarians and their staff to work efficiently harnessing the best of modern technology. People must be able to see and meet their elected representatives and to watch the Scottish Parliament in operation. Provision needs to be made to permit easy reporting and broadcasting of Parliamentary proceedings so that people throughout Scotland can be aware of its work and decisions.

10.5   Scotland's Parliament will be in its capital city. Edinburgh is the natural centre of government in Scotland. The bulk of the staff who will transfer to the Scottish Executive and be answerable to the Scottish Parliament already work there.

10.6   The Government are looking carefully at options available in Edinburgh which can best meet the criteria set out above. These will include new buildings as well as the conversion of existing ones. One of the options will be the Old Royal High School on Calton Hill. It is an existing building which has been widely regarded as the inevitable choice for the Parliament since it was prepared for this purpose in the 1970s. There are, however, serious disadvantages associated with the Old Royal High School. Public accessibility is poor - particularly for people with disabilities; there is little suitable space within the main building for people to meet their representatives; space is so limited that MSPs and their support staff would need to have their offices elsewhere; and there is an inherent lack of flexibility in the accommodation.

10.7 As part of the evaluation of sites for the Parliament, the Government are considering a range of funding options. The objective will be to secure suitable accommodation at a reasonable cost. The options include traditional funding, under which the capital costs would be met from public funds; using the Private Finance Initiative, under which responsibility for building the Parliament would be passed to the private sector; or some other form of joint public/private sector venture where the Scottish Parliament building itself would be publicly owned but where private sector partners would offset some of the costs of the project. It is not possible to say precisely how much the accommodation would cost until a final decision is made on where to locate and how to build or refurbish the Scottish Parliament building and on the most suitable funding option. Because of the range of sites under consideration and the variety of funding methods potentially available it is necessary to express the cost as a range of between £10m and £40m. The start up costs will be met from existing public expenditure plans.

Staffing

10.8 The Government intend that staffing arrangements for supporting the Scottish Parliament and the Scottish Executive should reflect the highest standards of public service: integrity, political impartiality, objectivity, accountability, recruitment on basis of fair and open competition and promotion on merit.

10.9 The Scottish Parliament and Executive will inherit responsibility for the staff of The Scottish Office and other Scottish Departments operating in Scotland. The establishment of a Scottish Parliament will not create a large additional bureaucracy.

10.10 Staff serving the Scottish Parliament will be servants of that Parliament. It is provisionally estimated that a total of up to around 200 staff could be needed. Functions to be provided will include committee clerk services, reporting of the Parliament's procedures, library services, as well as security, messengers, catering, cleaning, administrative and other support services.

10.11 As the Executive's powers will broadly include all areas of policy currently within the remit of The Scottish Office, its staff will be drawn largely from the existing staff of The Scottish Office and its Agencies. All officials of the Executive will hold office under the Crown on terms and conditions of service which will be determined in accordance with the provisions of the Civil Service Management Code – thereby remaining members of the Home Civil Service. Where necessary, the terms and conditions of officials becoming part of the Executive will be appropriately protected.

10.12 Established arrangements for interchange with other Government Departments will also remain in place as will present arrangements governing movement between the Scottish Office and its Associated Departments and agencies. These arrangements will give the Scottish Executive the support of a tried and tested civil service machine, and access to a wide pool of talent and experience. They will also contribute to fostering good working relationships between the Scottish Executive and the UK Government.

10.13   The Scottish Executive could need a small increase in staff over and above current Scottish Office staff numbers, to deal with new responsibilities currently falling to the Cabinet Office and HM Treasury; new responsibilities for policy development presently undertaken by Whitehall Departments; and to respond to the Scottish Parliament.

10.14   The Secretary of State will need the support of a small staff, as will the UK Scottish Law Officer. In both cases, this will be a matter for the UK Government.

10.15   So far as is practicable the views of individual officers will be taken into account when staffing arrangements are made.

10.16   All staff working in the new structure will continue to have access to trade union membership. The existing Civil Service unions will continue to be recognised for collective bargaining purposes and the present consultative arrangements and structures operating in The Scottish Office and its Associated Departments and Agencies will be adjusted where necessary to take account of the new arrangements.

Running costs   10.17   The total additional annual running costs - including salaries and allowances for MSPs, staff costs and accommodation costs - are estimated to be between £20m and £30m. These costs, which will be met from the assigned budget, are modest when compared with the annual current Scottish Office budget of £14,000m. The Government believe that, at around £5 per head, the annual running costs represent a first class investment. For the people of Scotland, it is an investment in democracy and in government which will respond to their needs and reflect their hopes.

CHAPTER 11

NEXT STEPS

11.1 This Chapter sets out the timetable for bringing the Scottish Parliament into being.

Referendum

11.2 The Government are committed to giving people in Scotland the opportunity to say whether they support the proposals for devolution. To that end, Parliament is considering legislation which will provide for a referendum to be held in Scotland. Voters will be asked whether they agree that there should be a Scottish Parliament, and whether they agree that such a Parliament should have powers to vary tax.

11.3 The Government believe that it should be the people living in Scotland who determine the future shape of government in Scotland. All those who are entitled to vote at local government elections in Scotland will therefore be entitled to vote at the referendum. Normal arrangements for postal and proxy voting will apply.

11.4 The referendum will be held on 11 September. The detailed arrangements will be similar to those for a General Election, drawing on the experience of previous referendums in the UK. Support for the Government's proposals from a simple majority of all those voting throughout Scotland will be sufficient. Counting of votes will be organised by local government area. Local results will be made available, but the national result alone will determine how the Government will proceed.

Scotland Bill

11.5 The Government plan, in the event of a positive referendum result, to introduce before the end of the year legislation to implement the proposals set out in this White Paper.

11.6 Preparatory planning and design work will need to be undertaken to enable the Scottish Parliament to be up and running on schedule, but no substantial expenditure will be incurred before Parliament has approved the principle of the legislation.

Arrangements for the first Parliament

11.7 The Government plan that elections to the first Scottish Parliament will take place in the first half of 1999. The Scottish Parliament will prepare for full operation as from the following year.

11.8 The timetable set out above will enable the Scottish Parliament to be completely up and running in the year 2000: a new Scottish Parliament for the new millennium.

CHAPTER 12

CONCLUSION

12.1   The Government believe that the proposals set out in this White Paper, which are an essential element of and first step in their comprehensive programme of constitutional reform, will be widely welcomed.

12.2   This White Paper does not aim to settle every detail of how the Scottish Parliament will work. It is right that the Scottish Parliament, once in being, should have the necessary room to evolve in its own way, rather than be forced along a rigid predetermined path. Wherever it makes sense to do so, the Government wish to leave matters open for subsequent decision by the Scottish Parliament itself. The focus of this White Paper has therefore been on creating a framework which will both safeguard the Scottish Parliament and give it room for growth.

12.3   The Government believe that the establishment of a Scottish Parliament on the basis set out here will be good for Scotland, and good for the UK; responding to the wishes of the people of Scotland for a greater say in their affairs can only strengthen democracy in this country.

ANNEX A

SCOTTISH PUBLIC BODIES

This Annex lists Scottish public bodies which have a remit which is concerned with matters to be devolved. It includes non-departmental public bodies (NDPBs), certain nationalised industries, tribunals and public corporations and health bodies. Both executive and advisory bodies are listed. It does not include bodies with remits covering reserved matters or any bodies with a UK or GB wide remit.

Executive bodies

The Accounts Commission for Scotland
Scottish Agricultural and Biological Research Institutes - Governing Bodies
  Hannah Research Institute
  Macaulay Land Use Research Institute
  Moredun Research Institute
  Rowett Research Institute
  Scottish Crop Research Institute
Crofters' Commission
Deer Commission for Scotland
Highlands and Islands Enterprise
National Galleries of Scotland
National Library of Scotland
National Museums of Scotland
Parole Board for Scotland
Royal Botanic Garden, Edinburgh
Royal Commission on the Ancient and Historical Monuments of Scotland
Scottish Agricultural Wages Board
Scottish Arts Council
Scottish Children's Reporter Administration
Scottish Community Education Council
Scottish Conveyancing and Executry Services Board
Scottish Council for Educational Technology
Scottish Enterprise
Scottish Environment Protection Agency
Scottish Further Education Unit
Scottish Higher Education Funding Council
Scottish Homes
Scottish Hospital Endowments Research Trust
Scottish Legal Aid Board
Scottish Medical Practices Committee
Scottish Natural Heritage

Scottish Qualifications Authority
Scottish Screen
Scottish Seed Potato Development Council[1]
Scottish Sports Council
Scottish Tourist Board
Scottish Water and Sewerage Customers Council

Advisory bodies Advisory Committee on Dental Establishments
Advisory Committee on Sites of Special Scientific Interest
Ancient Monuments Board for Scotland
Building Standards Advisory Committee
Central Advisory Committee on Justices of the Peace (Scotland)
Children's Panel Advisory Committees
Extra Parliamentary Panel
General Teaching Council for Scotland
Health Appointments Advisory Committee
Hill Farming Advisory Committee for Scotland
Historic Buildings Council for Scotland
Justices of the Peace Advisory Committees
Local Government Boundary Commission for Scotland
Local Government Property Commission
Police Advisory Board for Scotland
Royal Fine Art Commission for Scotland
Scottish Advisory Committee on Drug Misuse
Scottish Advisory Committee on the Medical Workforce
Scottish Agricultural Consultative Panel
Scottish Consultative Council on the Curriculum
Scottish Crime Prevention Council
Scottish Economic Council
Scottish Industrial Development Advisory Board
Scottish Law Commission
Scottish Police College Board of Governors
Scottish Records Advisory Council
Scottish Standing Committee for the Calculation of Residual Values of Fertilisers
    and Feeding Stuffs
Scottish Studentship Selection Committee
Scottish Valuation and Rating Council
Secretary of State for Scotland's Advisory Group on Sustainable Development
Secretary of State's Advisory Group on Scotland's Travelling People
Secretary of State's Advisory Panel of Economic Consultants
Secretary of State's (Electricity) Fisheries Committee
(In addition, the Scottish Executive will exercise Ministerial functions in relation to
appointments to the Rail Users Consultative Committee for Scotland.)

1 The Government have plans to lay an Order before Parliament to dissolve SSPDC later this year.

Nationalised industries	Scottish Transport Group Highlands and Islands Airports Ltd Caledonian MacBrayne Ltd
Tribunals	Children's Panels Horse Race Betting Levy Appeal Tribunal for Scotland Lands Tribunal for Scotland Pensions Appeal Tribunal for Scotland Rent Assessment Panel for Scotland
Public corporations	East of Scotland Water Authority North of Scotland Water Authority West of Scotland Water Authority
Health bodies	Common Services Agency of the Scottish Health Service Health Boards Health Education Board for Scotland Local Health Councils Mental Welfare Commission for Scotland National Health Service Trusts National Board for Nursing, Midwifery and Health Visiting for Scotland National Centre for Training and Education in Prosthetics and Orthotics NHS in Scotland Professional Advisory Committees Post Qualification Education Board for Health Service Pharmacists in Scotland Scottish Council for Postgraduate Medical and Dental Education Scottish Health Advisory Service Scottish Hospital Trust State Hospitals Board for Scotland

ANNEX B

OPERATION OF THE BLOCK

The Scottish Block

B.1   Changes in the size of the Block are currently determined annually by reference to planned changes in those English or English and Welsh programmes which are comparable with Scottish programmes. If planned spending on, for example, a comparable English programme goes up or down, an increase or decrease to the Block is calculated by reference to a population-based formula known as the "Barnett" formula. The sum of changes calculated by this means across all comparable programmes represents the change to the Block each year from previous plans.

B.2   This means in practice that as a result of each public expenditure survey the overall size of the Block for the following year changes, as compared with previous plans. Once the extent of that change is clear the Secretary of State has to resolve how to allocate the overall resources in the Block. While he clearly takes into account the changes which have been made in that survey to comparable English programmes, he is under no obligation to follow these.

B.3   Since these arrangements were originally introduced, the Block has been enlarged to cover more of the programmes within the Secretary of State's budget, and to cover new responsibilities transferred to The Scottish Office. The original formula was also updated in 1992 to take account of changes in the population differentials between Scotland, England and Wales since the original formula was established in 1978.

B.4   The Scottish Block and hence the Secretary of State's budget is not however funded entirely by grant from the Exchequer. It also includes expenditure funded by borrowing on the part of local authorities and other public bodies. There is not therefore a precise match between the size of the Secretary of State's budget and the amount of Exchequer funding for the programmes for which he is responsible.

B.5   The main programme which currently falls within the Secretary of State for Scotland's budget but outside the Block is the Agriculture, Fisheries and Food (AFF) programme. The annual changes in this are negotiated separately in the public expenditure survey.

B.6   Central government support for local authority current expenditure (known as Aggregate External Finance) is a large element in the Secretary of State's budget and is included in the Block. Local authority current expenditure funded from council tax receipts (the main element of what is known as local authority self-financed expenditure or LASFE) is not part of the Secretary of State's budget, and is not included in the Block although in recent years such expenditure along with other smaller elements of LASFE has counted towards the UK public expenditure control total – that part of general government expenditure which the Government seek directly to plan and control.

Changes to the Block

B.7   As described elsewhere in this Paper, the responsibilities of the Scottish Parliament and the Scottish Executive will differ in a number of ways from the current responsibilities of the Secretary of State for Scotland. Where these changes have financial implications, appropriate adjustments will be made to the Block. The opportunity will also be taken to make other changes to the Block in order to produce a more rational system of funding for the Parliament.

B.8   The main change from the present budgetary arrangements will lie in the treatment of the Scottish Agriculture, Fisheries and Food (AFF) programme. In future, AFF expenditure by the Scottish Parliament will be determined in one of two ways. A significant proportion of agricultural expenditure will continue to be devoted to payments under the Common Agricultural Policy schemes funded 100% by the EU, with the Scottish Parliament having no discretion in relation to the terms of this spending. This, together with expenditure on Hill Livestock Compensatory Allowances, which are also set in line with EU requirements, will be settled separately each year, based on the actual requirements of the programmes. The balance of present AFF spending will be taken into the new Block and annual changes will be determined according to the existing formula.

B.9   The budget of the Crown Office, which is currently negotiated separately with the Treasury and falls outside the Block will, in line with the devolution of the Crown Office's functions, also be transferred and will in future be included within the new Block. Similarly the external financing limits of Highlands and Islands Airports Ltd and Caledonian MacBrayne will form part of the new Block. The transfer of other functions, including those relating to inland waterways, Scottish ports and certain residual functions relating to the ScotRail rail services franchise may also require adjustments to be made. In relation to forestry, the financial arrangements will be agreed on a fair and equitable basis, taking into account the interests of UK taxpayers, in a suitable division of the receipts from the business activities of the Commission and an appropriate adjustment to the Block will be made in the light of these arrangements.

B.10   As discussed in Chapter 7, adjustments to the new Block will be required in order to provide the resources for meeting council tax benefit and rent rebate costs in Scotland.

B.11   The decision to devolve responsibility for non-domestic rates to the Scottish Parliament will also have technical implications for the Block, though the effect on the resources available to the Parliament will be neutral. At present non-domestic rating receipts are paid into the Consolidated Fund and The Scottish Office receives the resources back as part of its Block. Under the devolved arrangements non-domestic rate income will be paid to the Scottish Executive and the Block will be adjusted to take account of this.

B.12 The details of all of these adjustments to the Block will be the subject of discussion with Government Departments with an interest in each transfer and with the Treasury.

ANNEX C

HOW THE ELECTORAL SYSTEM WILL WORK

C.1   Each elector will be entitled to cast 2 votes: one for a constituency MSP and one for the party of his/her choice.

Constituency MSPs

C.2   Votes for constituency MSPs will be counted on a "first-past-the-post" basis in the same way as for elections to the UK Parliament so the candidate who receives most votes will be elected.

Additional MSPs

C.3   Votes for additional Members will be counted on the current European Parliamentary constituency basis and 7 Members will be elected from each of the current 8 European Parliamentary constituencies in Scotland. In the event of changes to these European Parliamentary constituencies in the future, the Parliamentary Boundary Commission for Scotland will make appropriate arrangements for the Scottish Parliament. Additional Member seats will be allocated correctively, that is to say that account will be taken of the number of constituency seats gained within the European Parliamentary constituency, on the following basis:

C.3.1   The number of votes cast for each party within the European constituency will be counted.

C.3.2   The number of votes cast for each party will then be divided by the number of constituency MSPs gained in Parliamentary constituencies contained wholly within the European constituency plus one.

C.3.3   The party with the highest total after the calculation in C.3.2 is done gains the first additional Member.

C.3.4   The second to seventh additional Members are allocated in the same way but additional Members gained are included in the calculations.

C.4   The Government intend to legislate for the registration of political parties so as to provide the means of identifying the political parties which will nominate the additional Members.

Printed in the UK for the Controller of Her Majesty's Stationery Office
by The Stationery Office Ltd.
Dd 293195 C50 7/97 (78158)